A SUFFOLK BOY

CW01645553

Published and Printed by

Leiston Press
Unit 1b Masterlord Industrial Estate
Leiston
Suffolk IP16 4JD

Tel: 01728 833003
Email: glenn@leistonpress.com
www.leistonpress.com

ISBN
978-1-907938-29-0

© John Cheney 2012

All rights reserved. No part of this book may be reproduced, stored in a retrieval system, or transmitted in any form or by any means electronic, mechanical, photocopying, recording or otherwise, without the prior permission of the author.

INTRODUCTION

I first thought about writing this book in 2001 when I was chatting to my son about the old times and the things I did when I was young.

"You should write a book, Dad", he said. A seed was sown.

Over the last few years, with his help on the computer, I have put my recollections down. These were the hopes and fears, the happy times, the sad times and the worst times, the troubles and the friendships of an ordinary lad growing up in rural Suffolk in the 50s and 60s, in a vastly different world to the one we live in today. I hope readers find them interesting, and I savour the thought that it may encourage others to undertake a similar project which in some small way may help perpetuate our Suffolk way of life.

During the course of reading this book the reader will find a few references to my lack of expertise in English grammar. I am grateful, therefore, to Mr Les Higgs, former Editor of the Heritage Coast Gazette, for dealing with these shortcomings so expertly in his editing of my manuscript. I recommend getting in touch with him if you are thinking about putting down your memories but find the mechanics of the language too daunting.

Thanks also to Leiston Press for their help and expertise in bringing this project to its successful conclusion, the result of which I sincerely hope you will enjoy.

Also Pat Ward from Aldeburgh for her help and advice.

John Cheney

Orford - 2012

IN THE BEGINNING . . .

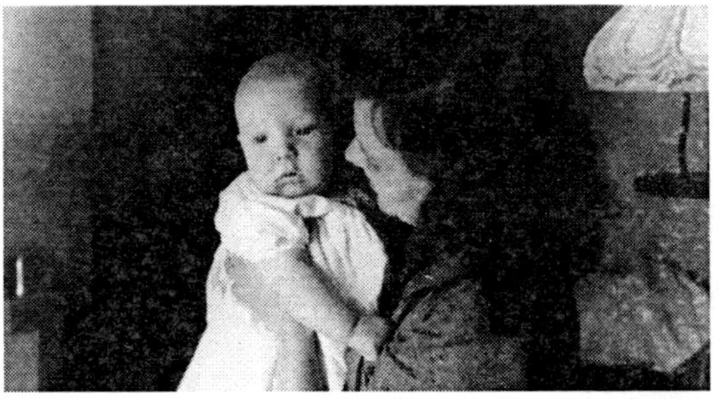

A few weeks old with mum.

My first breath of Suffolk's glorious air was taken on April 3rd, 1949, in Broom House, Sudbourne. My maternal grandparents lived there in a small part of the house, Gran worked there as housekeeper whilst Grandad worked at Orfordness. My parents, Ralph and Joan lived in Blacklands Farm, Sudbourne, which they moved into in 1947 from Newbourne, working with the Land Settlement in the glasshouses on their holding.

My father lived in Blacklands Farm before the War with his parents. They were tenants of the farm, then owned by the Forestry Commission. During the War, large areas of Sudbourne and Iken were used as training grounds for the army and a great deal of rusty military junk had to be cleared by the War Department before the land could was fit for use again. Blacklands was only 30 acres in size, the water supply was drawn from a very deep well close to the main barn. I believe it was sixty feet down to the water and one of my first memories was Mum going to the well and winding the handle to raise water.

All of us at the back of the house.

She warned me never to climb on top of the well, which had doors that flapped open as the bucket came up. This was the water supply for the farm and house but when I was about three we had mains water put on, just one tap on the outside wall near the back door. The tap and pipes had to be thickly covered up in winter because if the weather turned icy and it froze, all we had was water that we had saved in buckets.

This was taken by me when I had my camera, we were playing around, see leanto of Dairy.

Nowadays we take too much for granted, things were not always so easy. Our lavatory was down at the end of the garden close by the coal shed. It was a simple wooden seat with a bucket beneath and had to be emptied frequently in a hole which my Dad had prepared. For farm buildings we had two Nissen huts, more leftovers from the war, wooden pig styes, and a main barn made of corrugated iron sheets with a cartshed and garage built onto one end. On one side of our farmhouse was a thatched lean-to, where steps led down to the dairy room where my parents made butter in a milk separator. This was a device with a handle that turned the container to make the butter, a laborious and tedious job. Our butter-making machine was eventually sold to a Mr John Seymour who lived near Orford and was the author of several books on selfsufficiency, copies of which are still available from secondhand booksellers and on the Internet. Later the thatched roof was taken down and replaced by corrugated iron, the dairy was then used as a general store.

Me with the dog, Ben.

Perhaps my earliest memory of life on the farm was of Mum and Dad looking after the chickens which were housed in one of the Nissen huts on an early battery hen set-up. The hens were in cages, after laying, the eggs rolled from the front of the cage where they were collected by hand. The droppings went onto a belt which was turned by hand until they fell off at the end onto a pile. Hand power was used because there was no electricity, either in the house or the farm buildings.

One thing I can't recall is the time when I went off by myself and got lost, creating a bit of a panic. Mum told me that when I was just a toddler I went walkabout with my little wheelbarrow and our dog Ben. I set off across the fields and was gone some time before Mum realised I was missing. She searched high and low around the farm, fearing the worst, eventually extending the hunt to the fields. It was Ben's tail wagging above the corn that gave away my whereabouts. Dear old Ben had stayed with me until I was found, to everyone's great relief.

From an early age I can recall harvest time, the culmination of the arable year. The fields of ripened grain stalks were cut with a binder operated by wide canvas belts which sometimes snapped, necessitating a visit to Mr Woolnough, the saddler whose shop was in Church Street, Orford. Dad would take me with him and I looked in puzzled wonder at all the bits of saddles and canvas lying around. The shop had a leathery smell all its own, and when Mr Woolnough retired we had to go to Mr Easy's shop in Saxmundham High Street. The binder cut the crop and tied it into bundles called sheaves, which were then set up together by hand in twelves called stooks. When the whole field had been cut the stooks were collected and made into stacks. Then the threshing machine arrived and was parked near the stack. Power to the thresher was provided by a long belt from the tractor pulley and the sheaves were then hand fed into the threshing machine. The cats on the farm had a field day at harvest time as the stack was heavily populated with fat mice, which I used to chase, occasionally catching one by the tail and giving it to the cats. This was great boyish fun until the mice wriggled upwards and bit my fingers. Then I had tears in my eyes and blood dripping from my fingers requiring an urgent visit to Mum.

The binding type harvest did not last for much longer before the big red McCormick-Deering combine harvester arrived at the farm. This had its own engine but it still had to be towed by a tractor. The cutter bar was only six feet wide but it had a big tank adapted with a platform so that sacks could be filled with grain whilst on the move. The first tractor we had was a David Brown Cropmaster complete with leg shields and a pulley on the side that was used with a belt to work the small hammer mill. This was fixed in the cartshed with the platform to feed it located in the barn. Our other tractor was a Fordson Major E27N with a Perkins diesel engine. To a small boy like me this tractor was a monster as I stood at the front peering up at the Perkins rings logo mounted on the radiator.

FRIENDS AND OTHER ANIMALS . . .

Our farm animals comprised pigs, chickens and a Jersey cow. I watched Dad milking the cow by hand, as with each pull the creamy white milk spurted into the bucket below. The cream off the top was poured, still warm, over my Rice Crispies at breakfast, after the cow was gone Rice Crispies never tasted the same!

Dad feeding chickens, top of well in background.

Me, when I was a bit older, with the cow.

Now and then we had a large number of pigs, sometimes not so many, it all depended on the market at the time. We had Large Whites, Landraces and Blacks, the pig styes sited near the house were where the sows had their litters after the old boar had performed his duty. Later they went into the fields in pig arks, triangular shaped huts with skids on the bottom so that they could be easily moved around by the tractor, which was also required to carry their food and water into the field. Dad was on friendly terms with many of the main pig farmers in the area, amongst whom was Jack Hewett from Chillesford who also owned Butley Mill which ground up the cereals for pig and chicken feed. We often went there and I was enthralled by the sight of the gears working like clockwork as the belts and sacks came up through trap doors in the floor.

One day whilst I was with Dad in the fields, something in the sky caught my eye. It was a man floating down on a parachute. It turned out that he was an airman from the local American Air Base at Bentwaters, quite probably Mr Bruce, whose plane crashed in May 1954 after the fuel pump sheared off. He landed safely in a field between Orford and Snape and I recall seeing an article about him in the East Anglian Daily Times of 25th August, 2004, when he lived in Woodbridge after he retired as a Lieutenant Colonel. The article said that he and his wife were selling up and returning to the USA. He may not definitely have been the parachutist I saw all those years ago but the date was certainly right. I would have been about five years old at the time and I know that quite a few planes went down in this area, including one at Kesgrave.

My very first playmate was a girl called Maria Czerpak, whose father came from Czechoslovakia because of the war. Her mother was British and they lived in Sudbourne near the old blacksmith's forge in the Street, but they moved away when I was very young so I can only just remember being with her on the farm. I do remember that she was taller and a few years older than me and bossed me about quite horribly.

My next mates were Americans from a large family that came over here when Bentwaters and Woodbridge Bases opened at the start of the Cold War. I think they were Mexican-American and I can't recall their full names but I used to play with a boy who had the nickname

"Shirt Button", they lived in Blacklands Lane in a prefab bungalow called "The Birches". Mum and Dad had bought me an Austin Devon model pedal car with pneumatic tyres and a boot and we played with it frequently, pushing each other around the farm, the lanes and the nearby forest.

Me on the left, with shirt button and little brother Lena.

The house I lived in was semi-detached and our first neighbours were Claude and Lena Keer, who were keen motorcyclists and good friends with Mum and Dad. Lena would help out around the house and look after me when Mum worked on the farm. When Lena discovered mice in her house she put traps down and it was my job to empty the sprung traps by feeding the mice to the cats. She preferred me performing this task because when Dad did it he would tease and taunt her with the sad little corpses.

I suppose I was about six when they moved away, but they visited occasionally staying with old friends or Claude's brothers, but they always made a point of looking us up until the last few years of their lives. Lena was very friendly with Shirt Button's family and I think they kept in touch by letter for many years because Lena would sometimes speak of them on her visits. How bewilderingly rapid is the passing of the years, and as we grow older how much do we so wish and believe that we should have made greater efforts to stay in touch with those who passed through and enriched our early years.

Mr and Mrs Meadows replaced the Keer family arriving with two children, Catherine and Noel. They were both younger than me but Catherine was my companion as we played around the farm and I remember an exciting incident one Bonfire Night in November. There were no public displays then, "Health and Safety" was yet to be invented, and all the children shared their fireworks, which had been saved up for and selected after a great deal of “Penny for the Guy” begging and several other moneymaking schemes. On this particular Guy Fawkes Night we went next door to the Meadows’s and started the show, but a Catherine Wheel, not properly nailed on, dislodged itself off its post and screeched drunkenly away into our collection of fireworks, igniting most of them as it whirled around spurting rainbow fire. Rockets went off sideways, Roman candles, volcanoes, tuppenny bangers and squibs flew off in all directions as we scrambled for cover amongst this unexpected bedlam of blazing colour and noise. The fireworks show was short but the most exciting I have ever seen and we thoroughly enjoyed the rest of the evening talking about it around the bonfire.

By now my fifth birthday was looming and I nervously approached school days unprepared. After all, I had spent all my life so far living without a care immersed in the freedom of the farm, the fields and the woods, which to me in my world of innocence, held no danger, only the prospect of things yet to be discovered, things which still amaze me to this day.

Me with Grandad Pop.

I recall several members of my extended family. On my father’s side there was his father Robert, my grandad, whom we always called Pop. Grandad had brothers, I think one of them, probably Edmund, emigrated to Canada. Another brother was called Tom and lived in Kelsale with his son whom we called Sonny. I never knew my grandmother Kate as she died in 1947. My father’s sister Edna married Victor and they had a son called Barry, whilst Dad’s brother Harry married Emily and they had a daughter, Jane

Mum's parents were Percy and Kathleen. They raised five children - Ralph, John, Peter, Albert, and Joan, who became my mother. John was killed in the Second World War so I did not know him, but I was named after him. Uncle Ralph married another Joan during the war years, Uncle Peter married Hazel when I was just three, and they had one son, my cousin Richard. Uncle Albert married Mona when I was seven and they had two more cousins, Joy and Linda.

SCHOOLDAYS IN RURAL SUFFOLK . . .

In every little boy's life comes the big day when he has to start school, in my case it was at Orford Primary. To get to school I had to take the bus, a service run locally by Mr Friend's Garage in Orford Street. Mum held my hand to the top of Blacklands Lane where the bus picked up. I was most certainly set against going to school, my protests ending up in tears because I had no choice, I had to go. Although I had seen the school from the outside, it was with a feeling of trembling awe that I shuffled reluctantly through the big iron gate set into the brick wall, higher than me, which enclosed the playground. At break time we were handed out a small bottle of milk, one third of a pint, and at midday we were marched off to the canteen for a cooked meal. The 9d (4p) a day dinner money was collected for the week ahead on Monday mornings.

My first teacher, in Class One, was Mrs Simpson. Our classroom had a flat roof and was on the left of the school as you went through the gate. At break times we little ones had to use the small playground at the rear of the school, the front playground was for older children. Today we might find it odd that children stayed in one school from the age of five until they left to seek work at fifteen, but that was how it was before the War. Our lessons as five year olds were probably not much different from those of today - playing in the sandpit, drawing, cutting out, painting, singing and learning to add up.

For me the most memorable thing that happened in that first year at school was when I asked to go to the toilet. “No, stay in class,” said Mrs Simpson. But I really wanted to go and so I asked again if I could leave to go to the toilet, and again she told me to stay where I was. I could hold on no longer. I peed in my short trousers and made a puddle on the floor. Such accidents were by no means rare and the school kept a spare pair of shorts for these occasions, but I felt real shame at what had happened. Shame was a raw new emotion for me, something I had never experienced, as time went by I got over the trauma but I have never forgotten it.

In Class 2 my teacher was Mrs Joyce who lived in Creek Cottage, Quay Street, Orford, an elderly lady who may have been past retirement age but I got on well with Mrs Joyce and enjoyed my second year. During the cold winter months the classroom was heated by an open fire and we had strict orders not to go close to the fire after we came in cold and wet from playtime, but we still dared to sit in front of it whenever we had the chance. When the day ended I had to carry my books home and go through the day’s work with Mum and Dad. Every morning a big bag of books had to be hauled to school, then back again, and repeated day after day.

The unhappiest time at Orford Primary was when I went up to Class 3, taken by Miss Hellin, who later became Mrs Hawes. We were in a class of thirty children, sometimes I went weeks before work was set and marked. I must have become discouraged and then got into trouble, so I would think, “Why bother?” I was made to stand outside the room for talking in class because I was feeling fed up, and at other times I would get my knuckles rapped with a ruler. I was definitely not one of Mrs Hawes’s favourites.

In this class we had to copy work down from the blackboard, a tedious task that seemed to go on for weeks. How I wished the photocopier had been invented then! The class had a library, books could be chosen and read in class, but with only one exception they all had black and white pictures. Only one book had coloured illustrations and, as you can imagine, this was always the most sought after book. We also had lessons in sewing, some 30 seven-to-eight year old children let loose with sharp needles! Can you imagine this happening today? I tried to make a glove puppet but sadly it all fell to bits in no time at all.

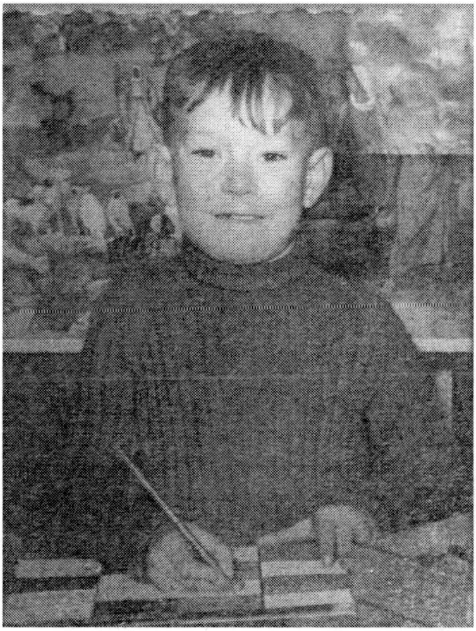

When I was in class 3.

The next year I was in Class Four with Mr Blowers from Leiston as our teacher. The classroom was the same one that I was in during my second year except that the desks were lined up in a different way. I got on well with Mr Blowers but I struggled with my writing and spelling which made lessons hard work. There were other teachers that we had at odd times, the one I remember best was Mr Innes from Wickham Market. He travelled to school on an unusual moped bicycle with the engine in the rear wheel.

At the end of summer term we looked forward to the long summer holiday. There had been talk of new classrooms and toilets being built during our six weeks break. The old toilets were wooden seats with buckets below which had to be emptied in a hole in the ground. Sure enough, when we returned to school three new classrooms had been built and new toilets constructed in what had been Classroom Two. We learned also that a new school was being built at Butley for children of eleven and upwards to which we were destined to go thus breaking up the old system of one village school for five to fifteens.

Each year the school held its annual Sports Day, a big occasion in the school year when all the parents could come and watch. The children were divided up into four groups of Houses, each being allocated a colour and named after a famous person in history. I was in Shakespeare House which sported yellow colours. Sad to say, I was never very athletic, always an "also ran", and I can honestly claim that Sports Day was not an occasion that I looked forward to very much, although I did my best in my own way, to uphold the honour of Shakespeare House. Sports Day was held on the playing field near the school and still is to this day.

As time passed I moved up into different classes until in my last year the teacher was our Headmaster, Mr MacMillan. We were taught in a small room with high windows but after just one term we moved into the very classroom I had been in when I first went to school and, unbelievably, I was sat very close to the spot where I had made a puddle in my first anxious year at school, an astonishing five years earlier. By this time, of course, I was one of the oldest boys and as the school bus was getting rather crowded, along with two pals I biked to school from Sudbourne, two miles each way on what were traffic-free lanes that we thought of as playgrounds.

Those two friends were Malcolm Keer and Adrian Proctor and we all enjoyed the bike journey unless it happened to be raining or we had a headwind to contend with. We usually played around on the road, making us late home, and we were even reported to the policeman who patrolled Orford at that time. He had a word with my Dad and I was in a bit of trouble. I remained in the Head's class for the rest of my time at Orford. Although Dad was very friendly with Mr Macmillan and they often went fishing together, their friendship did nothing to improve my command of English grammar, which was still at an alarmingly low level of achievement.

During the summer months we played school cricket on the playing field, the class being divided into two teams. I was not very keen on the game, especially as we played with a full size hard ball which hurt like mad when it hit you. In Winter football took over and any boy not selected for a team had to play hockey with the girls, who were quite brutal with their flailing hockey sticks.

The oddest incident that occurred involved a boy called Laurence Smy, a few years my senior, who apparently did not get on very well with the Headmaster because he poured hot tar over the wall outside the school house where the Headmaster lived. That wall remained tarred for years afterwards.

At last the time arrived for the dreaded Eleven Plus Exam. We all trooped into the canteen and were allocated individual desks. I was not going to pass and what is more, I knew it. The school held a final assembly in the canteen and at the end of our last day at Orford Primary our names were read out, we went to the front, shook hands and said goodbye to each teacher, who wished us luck in return. Then it was six weeks of glorious holiday freedom, after which I was off to Butley School. Mum, with Mrs Martin, spent the holidays employed by the Forestry Commission on backbreaking work weeding out very small trees, and although I didn't know it at the time, her wages would pay for my school uniform.

GROWING UP . . .

Me on my three wheel bike.

I was a quiet child, a bit nervous in some situations. I loved living on the farm and I would happily play around the various buildings, chasing chickens on my scooter, until I was given my first bike. My pride and joy was a cream coloured three-wheeler that took on a different appearance when I came across some old paint and brushes. The result was a mess that took a week to dry. My first twowheeler was a second-hand girl's bike, black with sixteen inch wheels that Dad bought at the local farm sale. Now I had to learn to ride, so Dad held the saddle to steady me and pushed, whilst I pedalled furiously before tipping over and grazing knees and elbows. But I mastered it in just one afternoon and then there was no holding me back, I was away. When it broke down, as it often did, good old Dad would be there to mend it and put it together again.

When Mr and Mrs Martin and their sons Christopher and William moved into a house in Blacklands Lane they called it "Pequod", after the ship in the film "Moby Dick" in which Mr Martin had a part. Now I had playmates close by since they lived just a bike ride up the lane to me. William was a bit older than me whilst Chris was a year younger. We had wonderful boyhood adventures going into the forest to climb trees or just messing about in the woods and fields. When we had a few pennies to spend we went to the only shop in Sudbourne, which sold most of the things needed for day to day living. It was close by the main road and was run by the Venners, who had two sons and two Dalmatians.

Early one morning we were awoken by the high pitched squawking of terrified chickens. Dad rushed out and found those two Dalmatians in the chicken coop killing any bird they could catch. Returning with his gun, Dad shot one of the dogs stone dead whilst the other managed to trot back to the village shop. Naturally this incident caused a bit of unpleasantness when the police were called and the second dog was also put down. Dead chickens littered the field and clouds of feathers blew about in the gusting breeze. Dad had the job of collecting all the corpses and Mr Venner had to pay Dad compensation.

Most of our chickens roamed freely about the farm. When the birds came to us as day old chicks they were put in sheds under paraffin heaters with big round reflectors. As they grew older they started to lay eggs which we collected and packed into boxes to be collected by a lorry. I only saw the two men with the lorry when school was on holiday, but I recall the older one was into horse racing. He gave us a tip for the Grand National, a horse called "Oxo", and it won in 1959 at odds of 8-1. The younger man was a motorcycle enthusiast who had been involved in several accidents and had broken quite a few bones. The last I heard he was working for Adnams of Southwold but that was many years ago.

After one year the chickens were let loose around the farm to become proper free range and to fatten up to improve the flavour of the meat. There was a cockerel or two amongst them so the hens sometimes hatched chicks of their own. Cockerels can get a bit aggressive and will come at you with heads down and wings outstretched. I was told a story by Peter Chambers that happened when I was very small and too young to remember. Peter, Dad and myself were out in the field when a cockerel came boring after me with wings out and head down. Dad chased the bird across the field until he caught it, killed it on the spot and plucked it before he got back to us. Mum would have cooked it for Sunday lunch.

Another incident which involved a cockerel happened when I was a bit older. My bike was lying on the grass and a cockerel came after me when I went to get on it. Grabbing an old polo mallet that was lying handy, I walloped it on the side of the head, whereupon it squawked, and jumped high into the air before landing and lying dead still. I ran indoors shouting, "I've killed a cockerel!". Mum rushed outside with me just in time to watch it stagger to its feet and run off.

That old bird never came near me again.

To some observers farm life can appear to be brutal, but to those of us born and raised in the country it's all just part of life. The first thing I ever killed was a rat, in view of the damage they cause few people would object to that. I was in the backyard when I saw this rat scurry across the grass. I grabbed a piece of wood, which happened to have a rusty nail sticking through it, and cornered the rat by the diesel tank. Two whacks were enough to despatch it, but when I looked at the end of the wood, to my horror the nail had an eye impaled on it. Farms are a breeding ground for rats and as far as my young mind was concerned that was one less. Later on I realised it must have been a sick rat because I was never fast enough to catch any more.

One of the main events that was held near home was Polo, held on the fields on the left on the way to Chillesford. It was a big event and the most famous person to take part was the comedian Jimmy Edwards from the TV series "Wacko!". Dad and some friends tried to set up a cycle polo event, he had the polo bike and the mallets and balls, but it did not take off. Later, a cow laid down on his bike and bent the frame beyond repair, so I ended up playing with the mallets and balls around the farm, which is the reason why a mallet was handy when I was attacked by that cockerel.

My first pet was a black and white cat called Smutty, who had to live outside with all the other cats, but I always made more fuss of him. Whenever the barn was cleared of corn there were always old sacks and scatterings of grain left lying around which inevitably attracted hordes of mice. This was a happy hunting ground for me and Smutty. As I pulled the sacks away the mice would scurry away and Smutty would pounce here there and everywhere. We got dozens of the little vermin. This happened on the odd Saturday morning and for an hour or so after the massacre I fed the mice to the other cats. Smutty always knew what was going to happen, his tail would start swishing when I said to him, "In the barn, Smutty!"

Me with my cat sitting on the car

Before mains electricity was laid on to the farm in 1962 we had to use paraffin lamps for lighting, until Dad got hold of an ex-Army petrol generator, but this worked out rather too expensive and so he acquired a Lister Diesel generator which he installed in the shed near the back door. The exhaust pipe was fed out through the back of the shed into a 45 gallon drum which was supposed to act as a silencer, but at night in the hush of the Suffolk countryside, you could hear the engine throbbing all over Sudbourne. A large belt connected to the engine turned a generator which provided DC current that would only light DC bulbs and this, together with paraffin lamps was how we carried on for years until the day came when we wanted to get a television, then the electricity had to be converted to AC current, a process that involved getting a converter.

Dad sought the advice of Mr Mattison who had the TV shop in South Entrance, Saxmundham. Every Monday he would do his rounds in Sudbourne, calling on our farm with charged batteries, square glass containers held inside a metal frame that were used to power the radio. To convert to AC we had a bank of 12 volt batteries providing power to the converter, then to the house. Without the engine running they would give us about three-quarters of an hour of TV viewing. Sometimes when the engine was running a battery would gas up and explode with a bang loud enough to be heard in the house. When we went to investigate the battery had acid dripping from a hole in its side, a dangerous liquid that burned skin and clothes. One of my jobs was to keep the generator fuel tank topped up, but I couldn't manage more than a two gallon can so I had to make several trips to the diesel tank to fill it up.

On Saturday nights we would regularly go to Aldeburgh Cinema, stopping by Wally's sweet shop at the top of Snape hill, or perhaps the shop near Aldeburgh railway station, or get something in the cinema foyer. I saw many of the great black and white films of the day, all the Westerns and especially the gangster films starring Edward G.Robinson, and Moby Dick with Mr Martin. When television arrived, though, we went less often.

At the end of August Aldeburgh holds its Carnival when a fair set up in the Slaughden car park. We came over to see Mr and Mrs Burrell before all going off to the Funfair in the evening. I had a magical, wide--eyed time taking in all the bright lights, the aromas and the music. I even won a china plate once, but I think it probably cost more to win that it would have done if I had bought it in a shop.

We acquired our first TV around about 1959. One of the first programmes I can recall was the Eurovision Song Contest with Teddy Johnson and Pearl Carr. This was about the time when Anglia Television was starting up so you needed two aerials on your roof, a big "H" for BBC and a smaller one to receive Anglia programmes. The coming of Anglia TV pushed up the demand for new televisions and aerials so, with commendable foresight, Dad bought an Austin Devon van with a bench seat that could accommodate the three of us, and a ro rack for ladders and poles. With this he went aerial erecting for Mr Mattison, and during school holidays I spent my days out with him, after Mum had made up our packed lunch and everything on the farm had been looked after, fed and watered. Dad and I talked about all sorts of things and I became a dab hand at unpacking and putting the aerials together whilst he was up the ladder fixing brackets on chimney or wall. I had the aerials prepared with coaxial cable joined up when he needed them. We travelled all over the Saxmundham area, visiting many villages and I still see some of the houses we worked on as I drive about today. Before the van arrived we had a Wolsey 12 with a roof that slid open enough for me to stand up on the front seat, my head outside getting a face full of fresh Suffolk air and tousled hair as we sped along. I loved this feeling but it all had to stop, of course, when the Austin van replaced the Wolsey.

Blacklands Lane was an unmade road and as our farmhouse was at the end, the milkman and the paper delivery would not come all the way up to the house. They were left at Mr and Mrs Tricker's who lived in Field Cottages. One of my jobs was to collect the deliveries from them at weekends. They had two children Molly and Marcus who was older than me, very much into motorbikes, and he gave me his old motorbike magazines. He also played football and gave me a pair of old shin pads, I felt like a proper footballer when I wore them. Saturdays were Mrs Tricker's cleaning day because when I arrived to collect the papers the chairs were on the table and the mats outside ready for a beating. The newspapers we took were the East Anglian Daily Times and the Daily Mirror which had cartoons that amused me. I had to ask Dad to explain what the political cartoons were all about, I recall many of them involved "Supermac", the Prime Minister at that time.

When I was about nine or ten, Dad got a job as a boatman working for the Atomic Weapons Research Establishment on Orfordness. When he worked the afternoon shift on a Friday, Mum and I went with him to visit my grandparents at Black Cottages. I played around the Quay or up on the river wall, but an alarming incident took place on one of these visits when I went off to play as usual, having been told to be back for lunch at 12 noon. There were other children playing around on the Quay who left one by one as the morning wore on. Eventually I was alone on the Quay with an older girl who suggested we go up to the old swimming huts. I went along but told her I could not stop long. When we got there we played around near the water's edge before she suggested we go inside one of the huts. I had a shock when she wanted to have a look at my willy. "That's not a good idea!" I thought, "I had better be off!", so I ran back along the river wall to my Grandparents, where I made it just as lunch was being dished up. "You look hot and bothered," said Mum, "Have you been running?" she asked, as we tucked into a lovely roast dinner.

In the Scouts, left to right, Me, William Martin, Gorden Caley, John Gouch, Paul Brown.

I first saw the Sea Scouts on Orford Quay and liked what I saw so much that I joined as soon as I could. Reg Partridge was in charge, we met on most Monday evenings and I stayed with the Sea Scouts until I turned fifteen. One day we sailed out of Orford for Havergate Island on a boat which Mr Partridge had borrowed, but the wind dropped suddenly and the boat was becalmed. We had no oars so we had to make our passage as best we could but it was very late when we arrived back at the Quay, causing a good deal of worry amongst our parents. The Sea Scouts from all over Suffolk had an annual camp every year but I liked the comfort of my own bed too much to persevere under canvas for seven nights. We also went to a Jamboree near Leiston that only lasted a day and I thoroughly enjoyed going to that.

For my tenth birthday Dad got me a secondhand .177 air rifle from the

Mr Partridge with Dad on the right.

Orford policeman's son, Randle. I made up targets in the woods and played there for hours, Dad would come along sometimes and set them up so that we could have shooting matches. My first pocket money was just 1/6d (7½p), which went up to 2/6d (12½p), but during the school holidays I watered the chickens and doubled my money to 5 shillings (25p). Mum did washing for a family friend, old Mrs Mannall, who lived in Long Row in the Street. I delivered her clean washing and collected the dirty stuff on Saturdays, for which I earned an extra sixpence.

We frequently went to Ipswich Speedway. A friend of Dad's, Mr Fison, was involved in the sport and had invested money to help get it started. On my early visits I was struck dumb by the clouds of dust, the noise of the screaming engines and the speed of my favourite daredevil riders as they roared around the dirt track enclosed by hard, wooden boards. Later I bought a season ticket, I kept many of the old programmes and still follow Speedway.

BOATS AND FISHING . . .

One day Dad said, “We’re going fishing!” I was about seven, we dug up some worms and drove to Iken Cliff where he had moored the rowing boat he had recently bought. “We’re going out for eels today!”, he declared, and sure enough eels were what we caught. All was well until they were hauled into the boat, slippery, slimey, squirming creatures as they are, they slid all over the place tangling our lines and tackle into contorted knots. We had lovely hot eels for tea that night and a fruitful pastime had been launched that would last for many years.

At Norfolk with Dad and Uncle Albert

Dad’s second boat was moored at Orford. Called “Churchman”, it was a beautifully varnished boat powered by an inboard petrol engine. We went beam trawling in the river, an old method using a long pole with metal loops at each end to keep the net open, the main drawback was that it occupied a lot of space in the boat. But it did the job and on a Saturday or Sunday we always cooked our catch for tea. Occasionally we went to the Norfolk Broads with Mr Mattison, the TV man from Saxmundham, who also owned a boat moored at Iken Cliff. He was usually on the lookout for a boat bargain and when he got wind of one off he went, sometimes with Uncle Albert and Auntie Mona.

Both Uncle Albert and Uncle Peter shared a boat in the river at Orford. These two told me a story about their grandfather, it might have been their great-grandfather, I can't be too sure now, but the story has stayed with me all through the years. This ancestor was a fisherman on a boat rather like the "Iona" which was beached at Slaughden for many years. He went long-lining in the freezing cold waters around Iceland, like so many East Coast fishermen did in the old days.

They were fishing off the Faroe Islands when scurvy broke out amongst the crew, a disease caused by lack of vitamin C arising from a diet deficient in fruit and vegetables. Scurvy was often found on olden day sailing ships, in its advanced stages there might be open suppurating wounds, loss of teeth, jaundice, fever and eventually, death. Grandfather ventured ashore one night and shot a sheep to bring back to the ship, but the noise alerted the Faroe Islanders who captured him and put him on trial for what was then a hanging offence. However, when he explained the condition of the crew they visited the ship and saw for themselves how dire the situation had become. He was released and a deal was struck that saved the crew - an exchange of fish from the ship's hold for meat and dried rhubarb, apparently the only vegetable the islanders grew.

Our next boat was larger than the others, called "Playtime". It was brought back from Norfolk and shunted into one of our old Nissen huts after Dad demolished the front wall. A small cabin was built at the bow, no more than a shelter from the elements really, and a new Swedish petrol engine installed. By now, Mum + Dad had got to know the Burrell family from Aldeburgh, and when the Boat Show was on at Earls Court in London, Hector and Louise Burrell went there with Mum and Dad. They stayed in the capital for a few days taking in a show at The Windmill Theatre, whilst I stayed with my grandparents at Orford and caught the bus from there to Butley School.

I never fathomed out why he was called Hector because his real name was Arthur, but I know the Burrell's were a family who had fished off Aldeburgh for generations and had been Lifeboatmen. They had two sons, Billy and John, and a crew member called "Rats Mower". This was another name I never figured out but Rats was always friendly towards me and I was fascinated by his tanned, weather-beaten features. Billy and John were both married, Billy and his wife had one child and another on the way, so I knew Richard and Caroline only as babies.

When we went to Lowestoft for the day with Hector and Louise we spent time walking around the fish docks looking at the trawlers, and ate lunch, always fish and chips, in the Fishermen's Mission. Best of all was when the fish auction was taking place, then there would be crowds of people, an exciting babble of deep voices, hundreds of boxes of fish everywhere and a smell of the salty sea that clung to your clothes.

When Dad had a problem with his fishing trawls we took them to Aldeburgh to ask the beach fishermen, John Burrell, for advice or help. On one occasion we took a net that was not working as it should have done. By now we were using otter trawl, which used two wooden doors to keep the net open when working. Those fishermen laid the net out in the street near their huts and pulled and tugged this way and that to get it to work properly, but we had to concede that some nets worked better than others and nobody seemed to know why. Sometimes we sat in the old Lookout on the beach enjoying the company of the fishermen and listening to their stories and adventures. Some Saturdays Mum, Dad and myself spent the evening with Hector and Louise, and in the summer months I took my model boat and sailed it for an hour or two on the yacht pond on Aldeburgh seafront. It's still there, I wonder how many generations of children, just like me, have played out make believe sea adventures there? When I returned to the Burrell's house in Park Lane they had some chocolate bars waiting for me.

There was great excitement the time we made the news. We had gone fishing for the day taking a packed lunch. We chugged out into

the river, lowered the fishing net and and sat there just making slow headway. After a time the engine was stopped and the net pulled up to inspect our catch. This time the boat came to a dead stop, getting nowhere whilst the engine was still running. Dad said we had better pull the net up, so he and Mum heaved mightily on the ropes but the net was so heavy it came up only inches at a time. When it finally surfaced they were
exhausted and it held a big round thing which Dad thought at first was an old metal buoy, but when we turned it over we saw it had spikes sticking out. By this time the boat was drifting in the river and was listing heavily to one side with the weight of this iron lump. "It's a mine!" yelled Dad, "Get it away from the boat!" He put a marker buoy on the net and cast it adrift from the boat. We made for home at full speed to phone the Authorities. If it had exploded we would have been spread all over the river.
The headline in the newspaper next day read . . .

TRAWLED UP MINE IN RIVER ORE

Mr Ralph Cheney of Sudbourne trawled up a mine when fishing with his wife in the River Ore yesterday. It is believed to be one of the small spiked type laid in the river by the Admiralty as an anti-invasion precaution during the war. Several of this type of mine have been trawled up in the past few years. The mine was marked by a buoy to await the investigation of a mine disposal squad.

So it turned out to be a small mine. It looked big to me! A few years after this incident, Dad and Mr Macmillan were fishing in the river when they brought up another one of the same type, but this time it floated well clear of the boat and although it was reported they never knew the outcome.

Sometimes, if we went fishing late into the night, the water sparkled with tiny diamonds of fiery light whenever the water around the bow was disturbed. I learned that this was caused by phosphorescent plankton near the surface. When I felt tired on these night trips I crept into the cabin and snuggled down under an old sheet with my head resting on a lifejacket. A long day, bracing salty Suffolk air and the gentle rhythm of the engine sent me off to dreamland in no time at all.

When the weather was kind enough we made an occasional sailing to Aldeburgh, tying up at Slaughden Quay so that we could stroll around the town looking in shops, chatting with friends, or perhaps for a change, sailing round to Iken Cliff, a favourite picnic spot on the river. When the herring were about we fished off the beach at Orford Ness with Mr MacMillan, my Headmaster, helping Dad with the nets they cast off the beach. They frequently enjoyed good catches and filled several boxes with plump fish. When they fished at night in this way I spent most of the night either asleep or half-asleep on the beach, but next day we feasted on the night's catch, which was often so plentiful that they were able to sell some or even just give it away. Dad set up a smokehouse back home at the farm, I just loved those bloaters and kippers straight from the smokehouse cooked in the pan by Mum.

Dad's next boat was the one once used by Billy Burrell off Aldeburgh beach, an open craft without a cabin. A new Lister diesel engine, very noisy, was fitted by Frank Knight's boatyard in Woodbridge, where Billy Burrell was having his new boat built. When the season was right I sometimes borrowed a dinghy and rowed up the river on my own to do a spot of rod and line fishing for cod or whiting. Our trawling expeditions finally ended when I was thirteen, the motor boat was sold and we reverted solely to angling..

BUTLEY SCHOOL . . .

The arrival of September heralded the end of the school holidays. I was off to Butley, dressed on my first day in a smart new uniform complete with badged cap which none of us boys liked very much, so caps were off more often than on. We had to catch the bus at the top of Blacklands Lane which then drove to Orford to drop off the younger primary schoolchildren, then on to Butley. On my first morning we were ushered off the bus into the playground where teachers took the new pupils into the main hall. Straightaway I was handed a box and told to take it to the DS Room. I had no idea what or where the DS Room was, but luckily, some other children had similar boxes so I shadowed them closely until we arrived at the Domestic Science Room where I happily completed my assignment. As time went on I got to know my way around much better, of course.

The new intake was led into the school Gymnasium where our names were read out and each group went off to their form classrooms. The Gymnasium looked very big to me, on one side there were wall bars and suspended from the ceiling were climbing ropes, I never did master the art of rope climbing. The teachers taught their own subjects, so that each class moved around to a new teacher when the bell sounded. Every class had its own form teacher who marked the register in the morning. At the age of eleven we were the “First Years”, next year we were the “Second Years”, and so on until you reached leaving age. During my first term the school looked and felt enormous after those early years at Orford Primary, and the 16 and 17 year old boys and girls looked very important, some were prefects with red or yellow armbands.

We quickly settled into school routine and the year passed without major incident. We had the usual classes, Science and Maths with Mr Blowers, PE with Mr Alexander, Mr Skopes the Headmaster took some subjects, and there were classes in Domestic Science and Needlework, which we boys never had. After the bus had dropped me off at Blacklands Lane I strolled home during sweet-scented, warm summer afternoons when the farmhouse windows were thrown wide open, and the radio got louder as I neared home, and always Mum's favourite programme, Mrs Dale's Diary, was just starting or just finishing depending on how late the bus was.

PE lessons were double periods in the Gym, involving activities like vaulting the pommel horse or scrambling up the wall bars, but no matter what the exercise, I hated every minute, including the shower afterwards. When the football season started I played in a T-shirt and shorts, with an old pair of football boots clamped on the end of my legs, not a problem in warm weather, but in the depths of a Suffolk winter I would freeze, immobilised. Perhaps I would not have sufferedso badly if I had put more effort into it but I was just not the type for team sports. I was quite happy when we had cross-country running, though, this was different because I could just jog around the course, take my time and get back for the end of the session. During the summer we had to try out different sports and if good enough could get picked to represent our house on the annual Sports Day. We played cricket in the summer and I was picked occasionally to represent my House, but usually as 12th or 13th man. I didn't mind, this was my favourite spot in the team, I just had to turn up, sit in the sun and watch the game. When it came to sport I was just downright lazy!

My first year at secondary school passed quickly, with the introduction of new classes, such as woodwork with Mr Allen. I made a few wooden bits and metalwork as well, and I liked the science classes with Mr Blowers. My first Butley school report was better than those I had from Orford. In my second year our form teacher was Mr Bantoaft, who took us for Rural Studies which included doing some gardening. However, by now I was approaching 13 years of age and had started to notice girls and seeing them in a different light. Some of the older girls looked very mature when they were on the playing field at break time or training for sports day. When this happened, word spread through the school like a forest fire and most of us boys would head for the playing field to watch them in their tight shorts and tops. I think the most prominent girl was Adrienne Cox, she excelled at sports, always won prizes on

Sports Day, and looked so delightful in her PE kit. Even when dressed in her school uniform she looked smart, with her fashionably back-combed hair. She left school around 1962 along with most of the other glamorous older girls, the girls of my own age never looked that good.

That second year at Butley simply flew past, we looked forward to the summer holidays again after our end of term exams in which my weakness at English spelling and grammar was exposed as usual. Our Third Year form teacher was Mr Blowers, our classroom was the Science Lab, where we sat at tables instead of desks. This was a year of ups and downs, I was approaching adolescent fourteen by now and I think this was possibly the year in which I grew up fast. There were four boys on my table, Roger Golsdsmith, Mike Cable, Terry Loveridge and myself. Roger and Mike volunteered as science monitors which involved putting out the equipment needed for experiments, after break or lunch. I helped them out with this occasionally because it meant that I could stay inside the school when the weather was cold, bearing in mind that we are now harking back to the winter of 1962-63 when the temperature plunged below zero for many weeks and thick snow smothered the fields and lanes. Up until then I had quite enjoyed playing in the snow but by the time that winter ended I was heartily sick of it.

English Grammar remained my bete noire. Our English teacher was Mr Martello, whom we had not met before, and of all the teachers I encountered during my schooldays, he was the one who terrified me. He was amiable at first but once he detected your weakness he would pick on you. I sat in class hoping not to be browbeaten again but it was always the same two or three boys, and one of them was me. I sat there shaking during his lessons, I could not remember the answers to his questions, and this made him worse. He made me look a fool when I knew I was no such thing. Before him, our English teacher was Mr Skopes, the Headmaster, and although I still had difficulty with the subject and often got things wrong, he certainly did not terrify me. By this time Dad had given me a 16 bore shotgun and after a day involving the humiliation of an English lesson with Mr Martello, I came home and cleaned the gun. It made me feel much better, perhaps a psychiatrist could explain it, maybe deep down I wanted to shoot the man who was giving me such a miserable time.

During this Third Year I was introduced to a hobby that would enthral me for years afterwards. Mr Blowers started a Photography Club, a room store cupboard outside the Lab made a splendid darkroom, the equipment needed duly arrived and in no time it was up and running. That summer Mum and Dad took us to Cromer for a camping holiday with a camera borrowed from his pal Ginger Rowe. Those two events kindled my interest in photography and so, together with my friend from Sudbourne, Nigel Leek, I joined the Photography Club at school.

The old ticket to photo show.

In March, 1964, Mr Blowers gave us tickets for a show at Ipswich, "The Magic of Leica", presented by Wolfgang Baumann. Our plan was to bike to school that morning, then bike to Ipswich after school and bike home again after the show. As fate would have it, it poured all day long and when it rained even heavier that afternoon, we decided to call it off. Perhaps it was just as well because the trip would have meant us cycling over 40 miles in one day. I was nearly fifteen by now and approaching the end of schooldays. My English was never going to set the world alight but I managed to achieve average marks in most other subjects.

The Photography Club shared an Agfa camera which was used on Sports Day to capture the action, and no prizes for guessing what was the most photographed subject. Of course, it was the girls in their PE kit! We produced one snapshot of a girl, Wendy Rees I think, in action over the High Jump. We sold dozens of this particular study! The Club was made up mostly of boys, a few girls did enrol later, which made for extra fun in the darkroom, though I have to confess, hand on heart, that my year group did not misbehave at all. After I left, the school divided darkroom time into boys only and girls only sessions.

When I arrived at Butley at the start of my final year, we found they had separated boys and girls into separate classes. My Form Class was put in the Rural Studies classroom with Mr Bantoaft as form teacher. Some of the boys found it easy to wind him up and as he had a bit of a short fuse, we had some pretty tense moments. We realised now that the most important thing to do this year was to get a good school report so I vowed to try harder across the board. I volunteered to be a Milk Monitor and, together with Trevor Phillips, we made make sure the milk was ready at the mid-morning break.

Our Music Teacher was Mr Underwood, but our class did not appreciate his fondness for classical music very much at all. This was the Swinging Sixties after all! For some unexplained reason, Mr Underwood gave us nicknames and some of these would stick. My mate Michael Golder was asked questions about Mozart but could never get the answers. Mr Underwood told him he was like Moses - lost. So Michael became Moses Golder, and still is to this day! My own nickname arose from an even more convoluted logic. Mr Underwood called me "Stock Car", because Dad had bought an old banger from Fred Brown, a Morris 8 with the registration AAH 1, with the idea of selling the number. Dad let me drive the old car around the farm and fields - like a Stock Car! Luckily the name did not stick beyond schooldays. My best friend at school was Derek Stephenson whom we nicknamed "Rocket", but sadly, Derek moved away when I was about thirteen and we still exchange Christmas cards.

I had plenty of fun with that old Morris. One day though, I was driving it on the track around a field during a downpour, so I decided to take a short cut across the field. I managed to get two-thirds of the way across before the wheels spun themselves into the mud axle deep. The more I revved up the engine the farther I sunk in until I ran out of petrol. There I had to abandon the car until Dad got home that afternoon. He had to go all the way to Orford to get petrol but when he returned and saw the state of the car and its predicament, I was in big trouble. We dug the wheels out and as we had no tractor, Dad had to use a very long rope attached to his own car on the track at the edge of the field. With the Morris re-fuelled we climbed into our cars and slowly, slowly, the Morris slewed out of the deep ruts we had dug. When we were back on the hard, Dad stopped but I didn't and banged into the back wing of his car, making two long scratches on his polished bodywork. This was the last straw as far as Dad was concerned, and I kept well out of the way spending the rest of the day in a draughty outbuilding. When teatime arrived, Mum called me in, and I dreaded to think what the atmosphere would be like at tea. I slouched indoors consumed half with guilt, half with fear, and quietly sat down. Dad fixed me with a look and growled, "I hope you have learned your lesson!" Mum must have acted as peacemaker that afternoon. After tea I went with Dad to rub down the scratches and touch up the paint, but the damage always showed, a permanent reminder of my juvenile thoughtlessness.

We were frequently reminded that we must do better. In this, our final year, it was essential to get a good report at the end of the year. In the senior years the School's sports teams went to play other schools at football, cricket and various other games. I was never good enough to get into any team but I was a reasonable cross-country runner. Mr Alexander told me my times were good and there was every chance I could make the School Team, he would let me know after the next training session. This time I took it very easy around the course so as to be outside the qualifying time. The last thing I wanted was to be bussed across East Suffolk to run around soggy fields, I wanted to stay in school in the warm and do some creative work in the darkroom. Another teacher was the Deputy Head Miss Gwen Dyke who took us for Religious Knowledge, one of my better subjects. I got on well with Miss Dyke, if you did as you were told she displayed a keen sense of humour. The best teacher of all was our History master, Mr Fincham, who from the Third year onwards transformed history class from a boring waste of time to an interesting experience, eagerly anticipated. His teaching skill helped push up my position in class at the end of the important final exams. I met him again at a School Reunion in 2003. Towards the end of that year the School Carecrs Officer interviewed us to try and fit us up with jobs. I wanted to work in a garage or something like it, a career in photography would have been my dream, but of this there was no hope. Dad was cultivating the land again and had bought a second-hand Fordson tractor from the Friston firm run by the two Brett brothers. Dad asked them if there was a job there for a school-leaver, and also tried at Church Garage in Snape. There seemed to be a possibility, but either way it would mean a long bike ride to work.

INTO THE TERRIBLE TEENS . . .

The Whiteways when I went to London.

Sid and Stephen Whiteway were the sons of a London taxi driver with whom I played when they came down to their family bungalow in Blacklands Lane. Just after Christmas 1959, I went to stay with them when they returned to their London flat in the family Bedford CA 6-seater people carrier after the holiday. Mrs Whiteway showed me around London, we visited most of the tourist attractions, including the Tower of London, where a Beefeater wrote a poem in my autograph book on New Year's Day, 1960. We went to 10 Downing Street when you were able to stand outside the door, but my lasting recollection of London was that it was very noisy. Every morning I was awoken by the sound of a horse and cart in the street, I think it was the milkman. Mum and Dad visited the Boat Show that week, so they collected me and we returned to Suffolk by train, the first time I had been on a steam train.

By this time Albert and Sophie Keer, Claud's Mum and Dad, had moved into next door. Their grandchildren sometimes stayed with them for a few weeks during the holidays and I became friends with one of the boys, Paul Timms, and we played for hours on my go-cart. Mrs Keer had a dog called Bella, I often took Bella with me for a walk when I picked up the milk and papers from Field Cottage. Mrs Keer was also very fond of cats, she must have had six or more.

Being a farm, we had cats as well, of course, they numbered thirteen at one time, but had to fend for themselves. We fed them with left-overs and scraps but

The old cat, Tiger.

if they were ill at all they either had to get over it or they died, there were no vets. They slept outside all year round on straw in the sheds, and sometimes a new batch of kittenish faces would appear, the result of what cats get up to in nature.

The gate between our houses was high with a large hole in it so that it could be opened from either side. When Mrs Keer fed her cats they heard the scraping of plates and scrambled to jump through the hole to get to the food. Occasionally we fed the cats to attract them into our backyard. It was great fun watching all those cats trying to squeeze through a hole only big enough for one at a time. I had a water pistol and when they popped their head through the hole I gave them a squirt, nasty boy that I was! The oldest cat, called Tiger, had part of a foot missing, I think it was lost in a trap, but even with only three and a half feet it could still run fast, and lived around the farm for years.

When I reached eleven I went to secondary school and games like Cowboys and Indians didn't seem the same any more, I must have been growing up! I still went off with Chris Martin to play in the woods, sometimes with our air guns. Now and then Dad came with us with his shot gun, and we hid in an old pig hut on a field to wait for pigeons to land before shooting them for our evening meal. Other times we strolled down to Orford. Our go-carts were made up of wheels from an old pram and any useful offcuts of wood we could lay our hands on. Go-carting was done mainly with Nigel Leek, we pushed the carts along the roads in Sudbourne. Nigel fashioned a canvas cover for his cart, we would run them down the hill just past Sudbourne near the forest on the Snape road. When we got to the top of the hill we listened for cars and if it was all clear, off we went on our rickety old machines. We got up a good speed and we usually got as far as the gateway into the forest. Nigel's cart always got a few yards ahead of mine no matter how hard I launched it at the top. Sometimes a car would come towards us and we had to veer off up the bank as they furiously tooted their horns. It was certainly not the safest of pastimes! In fact when Dad was told what we were getting up to he put a stop to it, but after a couple of weeks, when the fuss had died down, we would be off again. I did not go around with Chris as much because he was helping on Mr Jack Cuthbert's small farm, collecting waste food from local pubs and feeding it to his pigs.

Me with my bike and Nigel Leeks

The go-carts were abandoned when we got proper size bikes. With our new wheels we often cycled to Orford to meet up with Bernard "Tiggy" Green, who was in Nigels's class.

One morning just before Guy Fawkes' Night I cycled to Orford to meet up with some other boys, their names escape me, but I remember they had a box of bangers which they were letting off at random. We all decided to cycle to Gedgrave where they stuffed a few in a rotten tree. They blew up with a great flash and a stifled "Whoomph!", setting the tree alight, a classic case of unexpected consequences, so we all got out of there as fast as we could pedal. I had to get home for lunch and when I ventured back to Gedgrave that afternoon, the tree had been pulled down over into a field. I waited around, a seemingly innocent, curious bystander, hoping I was not recognised, but no more was heard about the exploding tree incident.

At last Spring was showing signs of overcoming the bitter winter of 1963-63, and although there was still quite a lot of drifted snow about, Nigel and I decided to bike to Aldeburgh for a change and spend a few hours looking around town. On the way home we passed Aldeburgh Golf Course and spotted a sign on the left pointing to the "Sailor's Path", which headed out towards Snape so we decided to explore this as an alternative route home. The track was still covered in snow and we hadn't gone far before meeting a man who said we would have to walk because we would not get through with our bikes. We carried regardless, not at all sure where we would end up, but after what seemed like a marathon we came to the end of the track at Sandy Lane. Having reached here we still had a five mile ride to Sudbourne and we were quite exhausted. I had to explain to Mum where I had been because I was late for tea, after which and I dropped off to sleep in an instant. Although that afternoon was a bit of an ordeal we still made the journey a few times afterwards, and one time we even cycled to Woodbridge, but only the once because the buses went there and that was much easier.

As soon as the shooting season started Nigel and I went brushing, or beating as some call it, on Firs Farm owned by Mr Hayman in School Road, Sudbourne. On a shoot, the brushers line up at the edge of a wood and walk through it making lots of noise and beating the undergrowth to send the birds flying up so that the guns can shoot them. It was an early start on a Saturday, we took a packed lunch and were given a small bottle of beer to go with it. The worst fields to brush through were kale crops because the leaves hold water and you end up with legs saturated and leaden. We were taken around on a trailer, bounced about on straw bales and at the end of the day we boys were paid out one pound, the men received more. A pound today may not seem like much for a day's hard work but back then it would pay for some of our photography equipment. The next Saturday after brushing we biked to Saxmundham to visit the Photography Shop in Market Square run by Mr Allen. We could buy a box of Johnson's developer containing two packs, one was mixed for film, the other for prints. Fixer also came in a two pack box, each pack making up about half a pint, the boxes cost us two shillings each, which gives an idea of how far that one pound went in those days. On one brushing Saturday Nigel and I were told it would be a short day and we wondered if we could get to the photo shop straight afterwards. It was indeed a short day and although we felt dog tired we cycled to the shop before it closed then biked home again. We were very keen on photography! I set up my darkroom in the spare bedroom at home. For Christmas, 1963, I had a Johnson Enlarger which Dad bought from Mr Allen at Saxmundham. Mr Allen gave me a pack of out of date photo paper, which performed just fine. Nigel also had an enlarger set up in his own bedroom and we spent hours in each other's darkrooms trying to develop good photos.

Once Dad got his full-time job as boatman our land was farmed by Mr George Gooderham, a farmer at Fazebones, outside Sudbourne, for the next few years. I didn't have much to do with the farming and the fields then, except when sugar beet was being grown. The seed was drilled and as the plants grew through they had to be hoed to about seven inches apart and to kill off weeds. Nigel and I did this on Saturdays and school holidays, being paid by the row. This provided us with extra pocket money some of which I spent on accessories for my bike, a speedometer from the Cycle Shop in Saxmundham, but when I tried to fit it myself I made a complete muddle of the job and had to get good old Dad to sort out the mess yet again.

Another source of extra money was black currant picking during the summer holidays. Mum and I cycled to the fields along by the Gedgrave Road, owned by Mr Gordon Barren who also cultivated apple orchards. We went picking along with a crowd of people from Orford. On arrival we were given a box with a handle in the middle and had to fill it level to the top. The box was weighed and if it turned out to be under weight we had to go back and pick some more, if it was over weight the excess was put into your next box and you carried on picking. I did this for two seasons, the first year's wage was two shillings a box, in the second year it went up to half a crown. I saved all my black currant picking wages during the second year because we were going on a camping holiday to Cromer. Before leaving we called in to see My Auntie Mona and Uncle Albert, who had just had a new baby, a cousin for me called Linda, who was covered in red blotches, much to my consternation.

Dad was going through the newspaper one day when he suddenly looked up and said, "I am going to buy two big glasshouses!" They were at Reydon, near Southwold, the Dutchlight type that simply screw together and had wheels which ran on rails so that they could be pushed along to cover different crops. Mum and Dad drove to Reydon to start dismantling them, some weekends I helped them mark up the glass panes and fittings so they could be re-erected properly. The glass was laid flat with newspaper in between each pane and brought home in our car trailer, luckily only a few panes were broken on the journey home. Mr Wright from Snape carted the main wooden frame back on his cattle truck. The next big job was to treat the wood with green preservative, something I was able to help out with when I came home from school. After that we had to rebuild the wooden frames and refit all the glass. When the glasshouses were completed and ready for planting, we put in lettuce, so tiny at first but they grew so quickly. One of my jobs was to see they were well well watered and when large enough they were cut, gently squeezed into plastic bags, and sent in boxes to to Stebbings the Wholesaler in Saxmundham, near the railway bridge. Moneymaker tomatoes followed the lettuces, which I watered and sprayed, and if Mum and Dad were out I had to adjust the window vents to make sure the tomatoes did not scorch.

Nigel and I discovered a pond in the forest, we believed it came about when an old army training bomb hole filled with rainwater.

So we built a raft out of old five gallon drums, wooden planks and rope. Our craft only took one of us at a time but we had hours of fun with it until a rust hole appeared in the bottom and let in water. Many a time I went home with wet feet. The bomb hole is still there in the forest but it has long since dried up.

With Mum and rabbit Molly.

I think it was about 1962 when Nigel decided he wanted to get rid of his pet rabbit. I asked Mum and Dad if I could take it on. I called him Moses, and he lived in his hutch in an old pig sty. After a while Dad wanted to have a closer look at Moses, and after turning him over and around, burst out laughing. Moses had to be renamed Molly! Chris and Will Martin had a buck rabbit so we put them together for a day or so and waited. A few weeks later Molly started building a nest in a corner of her hutch and a month later she gave birth to four little rabbits. This was the start of my rabbit breeding enterprise! My next rabbit was a big New Zealand White which Dad acquired from Mr Kent, the policeman in Orfordness. When we called to collect the animal it came with its own cage, and I called her "Duchess of Kent", because it came from Mr Kent and the real Duchess of Kent was often in the news at this time. We got several more rabbits from Ipswich, after mating them and rearing the babies into lovely little rabbits they went off to Wickham Market sale yard at Campsea Ashe. At the peak I had 35 rabbits of differing sizes, breeds and colours. The Duchess was a very good mother rabbit, rearing ten in her first pregnancy and four in the second, one of which I kept as my own pet, calling her Polly.

Collecting food for all those rabbits was an ongoing problem so I had to buy in rabbit food. Before long the feed was costing more than they could fetch at the sale so I had to cut back on numbers. When the Duchess contracted Myxomatosis Dad volunteered to shoot her to save her further suffering. I was upset over this, made worse because only days before I had found found Molly dead in her cage. After that I just kept a few as pets. Commercial rabbit-keeping, I had discovered, was hard work, getting green food and cleaning out their quarters was not as easy
as it first seemed to be.

My parents were always on the lookout for new opportunities and when a run-down cottage in East Lane, Bawdsey came up for sale, they stepped in. The place needed complete renovation inside and they eagerly set to work on their new project in their spare time. Sometimes I went over there on my bike to play around Bawdsey Quay. I helped with work on the cottage when I was able but it was clear this project was going to take a long time. Dad and Mr Martin even went to Evening Carpentry Class at Butley School, tutored by Mr Allen, my own woodwork instructor.

I had turned thirteen when Dad said, "Do you think you can handle a 12 bore shotgun yet, son? You had better have a go with mine!" He loaded it for me and told me to aim and hit the end of one of the Nissen huts. We were a good distance away so the pellets would just mark the black paint and we would see how good a shot I was. I took aim and fired but I missed and hit the muck heap to the side. This was my first time with a 12 bore shotgun, the trial showed Dad that I needed the next size down, a 16 bore shotgun. I never though any more about it until a few weeks later Dad looked up from his paper again and said, "We are going to look at a 16 bore gun for you!" So now I had my own gun and when winter arrived Dad and I went pigeon shooting in the woods at Sudbourne and Iken. I did not need a gun licence at this time, I don't think they even existed. As soon as I got home from school I changed out of uniform and dashed off into the woods near home to have a pop or two at the wood pigeons.

When we visited Mr and Mrs Burrell at Aldeburgh on a Saturday I walked down the Town Steps to the High Street to have a wander around the shops. I was growing out of my clothes quickly by now, my jeans were fashionably tight but they were so tight that I could just about get them over my feet, but getting them off again was a mighty struggle. I had a good look in the shoe shops and in the window of one I spotted a pair of chisel-toe shoes that looked so much better than the winkle-pickers that all the boys were wearing at the time. On the very visit to Aldeburgh I bought those shoes.

THE WORLD TURNED UPSIDE DOWN

I had a lot of time on my hands after leaving school and I spent most of it going out with friends. Dad had told me to take a few weeks off before staring work, wherever that might be. So I cycled off to Orford to see my Grandparents and meet up with mates to hang about in the village or on the river wall. It was agreed that I should start work when the new school term began in September. The best bet was that I would start at Brett's in Friston, a good bike ride away. Mr Martin warned me if I got the job to look out for the heavy traffic along the Aldeburgh road because this was the time when Sizewell A power station was being built. He was clearly concerned about me cycling along that road, but secretly I was hoping to get a motor bike as soon as I could.

That Monday started much the same as any other. I got up, Dad was at home because he was on the afternoon shift on the boats. We fed a tame pigeon that landed on the roof. I told Mum and Dad I was biking to Orford to see Tiggy Green, and after being told to be back for lunch at Noon, off I went. I played Monopoly at Tiggy's in the morning and as it was Aldeburgh Carnival Day we agreed that I would ride home for lunch and he would bike to my house in the afternoon, then we would go on to the Carnival. That was the plan.

When I arrived home the house was empty. I looked around the house and called out in the glasshouses but the place was deserted. I went next door to Mrs Keer. "I am sorry," she said, "but there has been an accident. It's your Dad. He is at Mr and Mrs Fly's." I ran as fast as my legs would carry me, Mum was there very upset, sobbing. Dad was lying on the ground motionless. Mrs Martin was giving Dad the kiss of life. A doctor and an ambulance had been called. I was in silent shock, just willing to ambulance to get there.

Dad was on the field working near Mr and Mrs Fly's house at Field Cottages when he stopped to have a chat with them. After a few minutes Dad crumpled to the ground. It was a fatal heart attack. Time seemed to stand still as Mum and I waited for the doctor and ambulance to arrive. The local policeman attended because it was a sudden death. The ambulance arrived at one o'clock, but in our hearts we knew it was too late to save Dad and after a short time working on him they said they were sorry and carried Dad to the house on a stretcher, us following behind, shaking, in floods of anguished tears. They laid him on the front room floor, I clutched his hand tightly and just cried and cried. That terrible moment is etched into my mind, I will never forget it. The undertaker had been called and he took Dad away. When Tiggy arrived I was still unable to control myself as I told him what had happened.

The days that followed are a sequence of blurred memories. Uncles Albert and Peter came to see us. There was much to be sorted out, the first being the funeral arrangements. I said goodbye to my Dad in the Funeral Director's Chapel of Rest when Uncle Ralph took us to see him for the last time as he lay in his coffin. The funeral took place a few days later. The Rector who took the service was a stand-in but he came over to talk with us which was a great help. Pastor Bugg from the local Chapel gave a tribute and offered words of comfort to me and Mum. The farm was rented so we faced the prospect of having to sell up and move. We needed work and a new home, but first we had to sell up. My safe, secure, happy world had collapsed.

The legal arrangements were put in the hands of Mr Fison. Flick & Son came to the farm, carried out an inspection and told us what was going to happen. Everything we wanted to sell had to be laid out in Lots on one of the fields, including the tractor and the combine. The glasshouses were advertised in the local paper, in the same way that Dad had bought them. The huts on the field went into the sale catalogue, the chicken run looked a bit shabby and when Flick's man said it would sell with a coat of creosote Uncle Peter, Aunt Hazel, cousin Richard and Uncle Albert all came over at the weekend to spruce up this chicken run. We got the creosote from Mr Bugg, the builder, and on a nice sunny day we got started. We made a good job of it but we managed to coat our hands and faces with creosote as well. As it was a hot day we knocked off to get a drink from the village shop run by Mrs Quilter and her daughters. When they saw us they couldn't believe what had happened, we had red blotches and blisters on our faces. They made a great fuss of us and smeared our faces with cream before sending us off home with the drinks.

When the day of the sale arrived we drove the car and tractor out onto the field with everything else and left. We did not want to be around when all we had was being auctioned off, so we went to the Grandparents in Orford for the day, hoping the car would be bought by a stranger so we would not see it being driven around our village. The sale raised a bit of cash with the car and tractor fetching the most. The car was sold to George Phillips, a colleague of Dad's on the boats. The glasshouses were sold through the paper a bit later. We still had the tomatoes growing in them, so we harvested the crop and sold it to Stebbings. This cleared the farm, all we needed now was an income and a home.

Orford Primary School was advertising for an assistant cook, so Mum applied and got the job. She worked with Mrs Goddard who had cooked my dinners when I was at Orford Primary. The cottage at Bawdsey had to be sold as it stood, it still needed a lot of work to complete the renovations. The sale was in the hands of Mr Fison and as the site had to be cleared up, Mr Mattison offered to help in his Morris Traveller Estate. He hitched our trailer on to his towbar and the three of us went over to Bawdsey to clean up. We filled the car, the trailer and the roof rack with our things before making our way home. The house was now ready to go on the market. Mr George Bantoaft lived in Pump Street, Orford, and knew Dad very well. He tipped us off about a two-bed terraced house, Number 96 Castle Lane, Orford, when it came up for sale. It had no mains water, bathroom and toilet and needed a complete rewire. At the back was a small garden with a coal shed and a wash house with old-fashioned copper. The lavatory was near the coal shed, consisting of a rusty bucket which had to be emptied on the vegetable garden over the road. The front door opened onto the road, so much different to the farm. The house at Bawdsey was sold and with the proceeds we bought 96 Castle Lane. Uncle Peter drew up plans for a small kitchen and bathroom.

What I needed now was a job, this had been put on hold until after the farm sale. Uncle Peter asked at the Orford Garage, saying it would be ideal as it was very close to our new home. As luck would have it, there was a job vacancy so I started working life on 5th October, 1964. To start with I was the petrol pump attendant on the forecourt, petrol at that time was 4/6d to 5/3d per gallon, 23p to 26p in decimal currency, half that price being tax. I also had to repair cycle punctures and keep the workshop tidy. Somehow I always managed to get in a mess, covered in dirt and oil from head to toe. The first thing I noticed about working life was the noise in the workshop, all the benches were metal and the mechanics made such a loud banging and clattering as they worked. As we were still living in Sudbourne, it was a bike ride for me to get to work at 8am, Mum started a bit later in the school kitchen.

On Friday nights we stayed over at my Grandparents in Black Cottage for the weekend so that we could work on 96 Castle Lane. Friday evening my grandfather, Uncle Peter and myself went along to the Jolly Sailor in Quay Street. There I could have a pint of Adnams bitter, although I was still underage at fifteen. We visited Uncle Albert and Aunt Mona for tea on Saturday. I worked at the garage on Saturday mornings but in the afternoon I helped out at our new house, along with both aunts and uncles we got the decorating done. Uncle Albert rewired the house for electricity.I thank God for the good family I had around me.

That Christmas was our first without Dad, we spent it quietly at Orford. I only had Christmas Day and Boxing Day off from work, but Mum had longer because the school was closed. We still lived at Sudbourne for the next few weeks but the long-awaited day came when 96 Castle Lane was ready and we moved into our new home in February, 1964. The removal lorry was the Wright Brothers' cattle truck, the one we had used to pick up the glasshouses, and it may even have taken some of our pigs to market many years before. I had to book the morning off work as we moved on a Saturday. The truck arrived early, washed and cleaned, and we loaded up all the possessions we had, most of them having been sold on sale day. Everything went in one load, I was relegated to the back of the truck where I could only see out through a tiny slit window. I had seen this same lorry filled with pigs and cattle looking out of the very window I was staring through. Perhaps they were wondering what their fate was going to be, I was certainly thinking what the future might hold for me and Mum. As the truck started up and began to move away I watched as the farmhouse gradually recede into the distance. My eyes filled with tears and I knew that my boyhood was over, I had left it at Blacklands.

The truck soon arrived at Orford and for a few hours we were busy moving in. The lorry left and we settled down to sorting ourselves out. Water had to be fetched from the pump outside the village shop, but I only had to do this for a day or so as Mr Stan Green next door had a tap in his outhouse which he let us use. I still had to dig a hole in the garden over the road to empty the toilet bucket. The garden went with the house and was meant for vegetable growing. That Easter, near my 16th birthday, mains water was laid on, a water tap outside the front door, Uncle Albert run a pipe under our front room wooden floor and connected it up to a tap indoors. Running water inside the house at last, even if it was icy cold! Uncle Peter's plans for the kitchen and bathroom were ready and work started. On my 16th birthday I received a welcome pay rise.

The years have rolled relentlessly onward, my Uncles, Aunts apart from aunt Mona, and my dear Mum have all died. A new generation has replaced them including my own son Jonathan. On Mum's side we have cousin Linda's three children, Ben, Joe and Meg, and Joy's two boys Jack and Harry. On Dad's side, my cousin Barry has died but he left two daughters, Carina and Michelle. Also my play mate Chris Martin is no longer with us.

A SUFFOLK BOY